Terms and Conditions

LEGAL NOTICE

The Publisher has strived to be as accurate and complete as possible in the creation of this report, notwithstanding the fact that he does not warrant or represent at any time that the contents within are accurate due to the rapidly changing nature of the Internet.

While all attempts have been made to verify information provided in this publication, the Publisher assumes no responsibility for errors, omissions, or contrary interpretation of the subject Matter herein. Any perceived slights of specific persons, peoples, or organizations are unintentional.

In practical advice books, like anything else in life, there are no guarantees of income made. Readers are cautioned to reply on their own judgment about their individual circumstances to act accordingly.

This book is not intended for use as a source of legal, business, accounting or financial advice. All readers are advised to seek services of competent professionals in legal, business, accounting and finance fields.

You are encouraged to print this book for easy reading.

Table Of Contents

Foreword

Chapter 1:
Intro To Outsourcing

Chapter 2:
Learn How To Use Freelance Sites Like Elance

Chapter 3:
The Importance Of Seeking Value Over Price When You Can

Chapter 4:
Make Sure To Qualify The Person You're Sending Work To

Chapter 5:
Choose Projects To Outsource Carefully

Chapter 6:
Make Sure The Project Specs Are Defined And Understood

Chapter 7:
Keep Good Lines Of Communication Open

Chapter 8:
Check Project Progress Regularly

Chapter 9:
Make Sure To Provide Helpful Feedback

Chapter 10:
The Dangers Of Not Understanding How To Outsource Correctly

Wrapping Up

Foreword

Outsourcing is really catching on as a popular tool to use when time and manpower is a problem within a particular group, work environment, or company. There are ways in this book for you to learn how to be a master outsourcer.

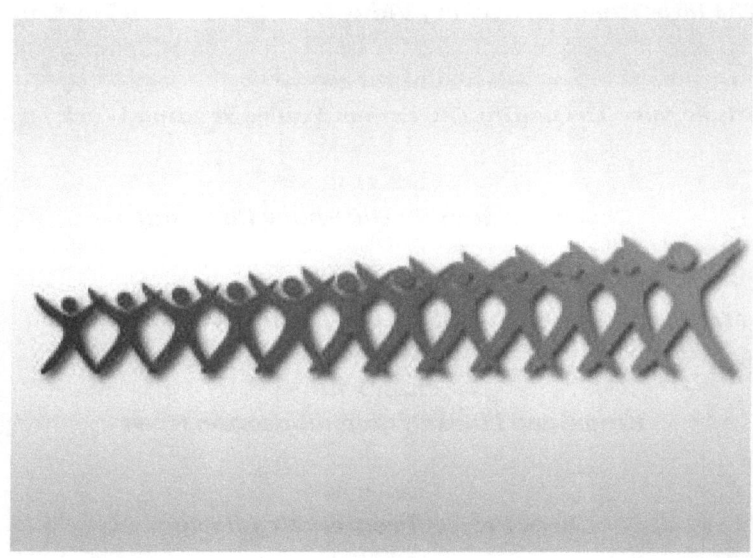

Outsourcing Your Life
Avoid The Pitfalls Of Poor Outsourcing Practices And Maximize Output

Chapter 1:
Intro To Outsourcing

Synopsis

Basically outsourcing is the use of outside sources to get particular aspects of a job done within a certain time frame. Though these jobs are normally handled within the company frame, however due to various reasons the option of out sourcing is sought. Jobs like call centre services, email services, payroll services and others are the most popular for out sourcing.

What Is It

One of the most popular reasons companies use out sourcing facilities is because the cost incurred is much less if compared to actually having to hire in house.

When out sourcing services are used the company can avoid paying other costs like overtime, salaries, medical benefits and others. The out sourcing cost is done at one specific fee without any other expenses incurred.

Out sourcing also allows a company to stay focused on their core business without having to oversee other aspects of their business. This is left to the professional services of an out sourcing company. Therefore the resources of the company can now be fully utilized for the enhancement of its core business.

Another advantage of out sourcing is that if and when a company decides to expand into other countries, the foundations that are required to be established and implemented can be done throughout sourcing.

This is wise as a good outsourcing company will have the necessary infra structure to get the relevant tasks done. Also most out sourcing companies have the resources and business needs to merit monetary investments for certain tools that are needed for its particular service.

Most companies today find this arrangement easy and fuss free not to mention cost effective, thus the emerging popularity of out sourcing.

Chapter 2:

Learn How To Use Freelance Sites Like Elance

Synopsis

In recent years there is a significant increase in out sourcing companies emerging around the world. The demand for the services of such companies is rising and fast. The services provided by out sourcing companies are becoming somewhat of a necessity and a popular option available today.

Freelance Sites

There are several out sourcing companies which build their client portfolios based on their significant success rate and the satisfaction of their customers. One such company is Elance.

This company provides the necessary services that allow companies to facilitate posting of projects, assessing the bidders, reviewing the qualification, ratings, portfolios, and skills. As the onetime fee charged for this service is very low, companies are more than happy to use this as a tool to get on with other more pressing matter that require the bulk of their time and effort.

Some of the services provided by the out sourcing companies include web development, programming, creative design, multimedia production, writing, search engine optimization, content translations and research.

Using out sourcing services also allows a company to use all the business tools available but on an online platform rather than having to provide onsite facilities.

Outsourcing services also provide a wider and more interchangeable way of getting the job done. Time lines are also strictly followed as these out sourcing companies depend heavily on their reputations to ensure they stay in business. Therefore the check and balance style is very much the business style. This then creates the opportunity for the customers to be able to view the work in progress and on demand.

There is also no need to have permanent staff which incurs unnecessary costs, especially when the work load style is seasonal. Using the out sourcing services almost always lessens the burden on the company to provide the frame work that may not always be utilized to its optimum.

Chapter 3:
The Importance Of Seeking Value Over Price When You Can

Synopsis

Cost is always an important factor in any scenario, be it on a personal level or on a much bigger platform. Being cost effective is very important to the progress and success of a company. When the issue of cost is considered, it is not always prudent or wise to go for the cheapest option.

Value

There are several reasons as to why it is sometime wiser to go for the more expensive option. Going cheap is not always wise because in most cases, one gets the services and quality one pays for. Therefore opting for the cheapest pick can mean substandard and unreliable quality and delivery.

There are some things that are simply worth paying for, as the high cost ensures the quality and service is always at its best. Paying more and getting the best is definitely worth the cost especially when reputations, businesses, and quality standards are all on the line. People should be made aware of the fact that good services and quality come at a price.

It may not always be so, but most time when something is termed expensive it is more than likely worth the price. Professionalism comes at a cost, therefore when deciding on a company to outsource work to the integrity and reputation of the company is often scrutinized thoroughly before a commitment is made.

Companies often charge according to their merits and if their skills and services are above reproach, most customers will not begrudge the expensive price tag because they are confident in the services paid for.

Also with making the choice of value over price, there is an assurance of peace of mind in knowing that the cost incurred is well worth it. Peace of mind for most is priceless and if it can be satisfactorily provided for, no cost is too much.

Chapter 4:
Make Sure To Qualify The Person You're Sending Work To

Synopsis

As more and more companies are choosing to outsource the bulk of what they consider time consuming or unnecessary use of resources, there are quite a few elements to consider.

Can They Do It

The first of course is the fact that it is a cheaper option than to hire in house staff which would in turn incur a lot of hidden costs. However in using the out sourcing option one must consider carefully the set back that might occur should a wrong choice be made in terms of the out sourcing company chosen.

Ensuring the expertise of the chosen out sourcing company is very important and the first of many steps to consider. The talent and technological skills of the out sourcing company must match the requirements of the "customer."

Trying the various out sourcing companies until a suitable match is found is normally practiced. When an out sourcing company is chosen based on its merits and reputation, further enquiries must be made to ascertain if the company is capable of handling the specific work required of it.

If this is not clearly out lined there is a danger to having to either re outsource the work at considerable cost and loss of time or to have a new out sourcing company chosen.

Sometimes besides the more obvious requirements, there can be some other items that need to be explored before making a commitment to outsource the work to a chosen company. Some companies may require the flexibility of the hiring exercise to be

clearly stated and understood by both parties. Hiring specialist without having to keep them on a retainer is especially good for companies that don't have consistent business to outsource. Therefore it is of upmost importance to ensure both parties' needs are adequately met before the out sourcing work is awarded.

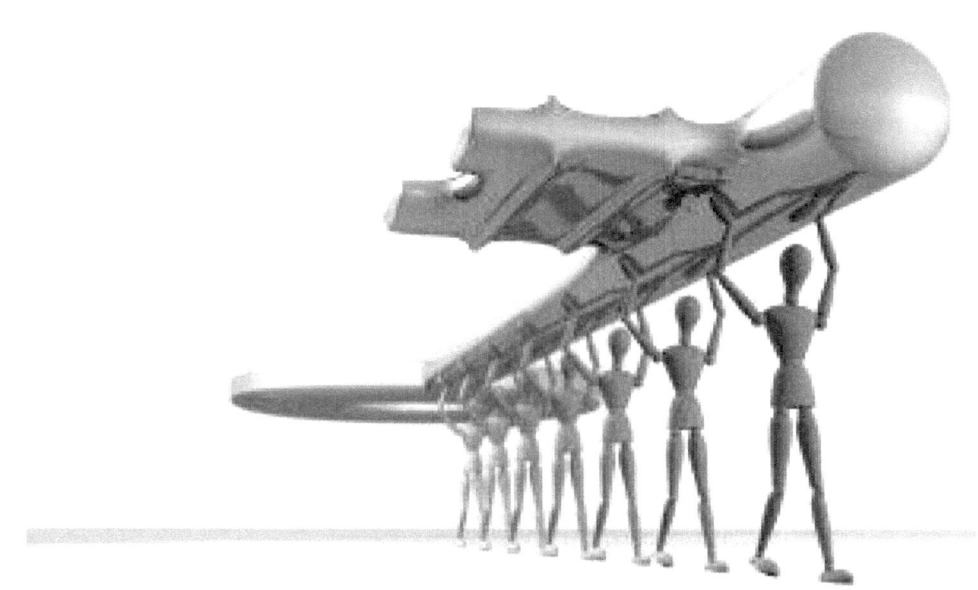

Chapter 5:
Choose Projects To Outsource Carefully
Synopsis

Simply deciding to outsource anything and everything to another company can prove to be quite a foolish decision to make. Besides the obvious reasons like cost and time lines there are also some other more sensitive issues that should be addressed when deciding to outsource.

Pick Carefully

One particular issue to consider is the sensitivity of the material given for out sourcing. If the contents of the out sourcing material is leaked to a competitor of the customer that a lot of serious damage can occur in terms of loss of business or sometimes even business secrets.

The ethical standards of an out sourcing company would have to be closely scrutinized if there is a need to outsource sensitive material. There has to be some sort of confidentially clause that ties the out sourcing company to be held responsible for any information divulged to other sources.

Unfortunately today's business world practices are not very ethical or straight forward, thus the need to be extremely discerning when choosing the out sourcing company. The employees of the out sourcing company must be duty bound to keep all information confidential.

Some projects don't require much thought when deciding to use the services of an out sourcing company, while there are some project that do, especially when it involves new inventions, new innovative ideas, new product launches, new designs, new systems and many more. All these are highly sensitive and cost conscious and if this information falls into the wrong hands the damage done can be monumental and irreversible.

There are also some projects that require the highest level of technically sound understanding. If the decision to outsource is made then this information must be first explained and understood before the work is awarded. This needs to be done to ensure the time lines tagged to the exercise is not delayed or worse still to find at the end of a given time frame the out sourced company did not complete the task awarded accurately and on time.

Chapter 6:
Make Sure The Project Specs Are Defined And Understood

Synopsis

When an out sourcing company is hired to perform a specific exercise or task, there need to be clear understanding on both sides as to the expectations and material involved. A lot of future problems can be avoided if this is made clear from the onset of the partnership, because in effect it is a partnership of sorts.

Putting It To Work

Being as clear as possible to what is expected in terms of accomplishments is necessary and important. It would be prudent to take the time to communicate the projects at hand and further ensure the essence of the intended project is clearly understood.

Expectations, fees incurred and time lines should be all clearly addressed and agreed upon before a partnership is formed. The talent used by the out sourcing company must be up to the requirements of the customer as each project specs can differ greatly thus the need to have a very diversified group of people available for each project at any given time.

If the project specs require a lot of technical understanding then the relevant out sourcing company has to be sought. A thorough discussion on the expectation for either party must be clearly defined and agreed upon. It would be a tremendous waste of resources and valuable time if the end product does not match the requirements of the customer. This can not only cause the progress of the hiring company to stall but could also end up causing other negative repercussion like loss of huge market shares of a potential customer base.

All these are important as the exercise of out sourcing is no longer just about cutting cost but is also about how to get things done more efficiently, quickly and competitively to ensure a larger share of the customer percentage.

Chapter 7:
Keep Good Lies Of Communication Open

Synopsis

Strong communication is the key to keeping the relationship between the out sourcing company and its customer comfortable and beneficial to both parties. If there is a good line of communication established between the two entities then and only then will the partnership be a successful one.

Communicate

When there is a good open line of communication established, both parties can avoid any unnecessary setbacks as constant enquiries can be made on the various aspects and progress of the task at hand. Direct reports and check and balance systems can be firmly established without having to go through a lot of "red tape" that cause unnecessary delays and frustrations.

The key to keeping both parties from being unduly anxious is to establish a good open communication line between the two. This also helps to contribute to the building of trust towards both parties.

The line of open communication must also consist of both parties being able to be good listeners as well as communicators. This will prove to be valuable in understanding the requirements and working towards the needs of the customer to ensure the end product is satisfactorily achieved.

With the establishment of good communication between the two parties, there hence creates the opportunities for honest communication and the exchange of ideas. This added source of positive input could also help to further contribute to the success of the project and partnership.

As most out sourcing companies are quite well informed in their various fields, they could also assist the customer with suggesting various innovative ideas that would benefit and perhaps enhance the customers business further.

As communication has always been known to be the weakest part of any organization or partnership, everyone involved should try to go the extra mile in the effort to ensure all material communicated is thoroughly understood and executed accordingly.

Chapter 8:
Check Project Progress Regularly

Synopsis

Every project requires a lot of thought and processes to make it a success. Some of these processes should include a good check and balance system to ensure the success reached is definite.

Check In

When the said project involves a few people the idea of checking up on everyone frequently can be quite a hassle though very necessary. Therefore it is wise to have a system in place that can keep and coordinate all progress clearly and efficiently. These systems used should be customized to meet the requirement of the project it is assessing.

Having a check and balance system in place also allows all those connected to the project to be able to view its progress as a whole or in individual sections. Viewing the individual sections is equally important to ensure when all the various sections are combined there will not be any problems it term of the overall results.

Frequent checks also ensure the relevant progress of each part or section is kept to its time line and specific requirements. If at any time either of these elements are not according to the fit of the entire project then the necessary changes can be made. Hence there is no need to worry about not arresting any particular problem in time and certainly not having to cope with the negative "snowball" effect caused by wrongly managed sections.

Regular checking exercises also help to boost the confident and commitment levels of all those participating in the project. It keeps

everyone in the "know or loop" and thus all participants will be weary of not keeping up to their particular sections.

Another good reason to implement a good check and balance system is to ensure the budgeting is kept to the original amount allotted. Any over runs can be immediately identified and addressed. This will ensure costs don't escalate unnecessarily.

Chapter 9:
Make Sure To Provide Helpful Feedback

Synopsis

Out sourcing company often help their client with useful information that they think might help further enhance the efficiency of the company project. The reason they are able to do this is because most out sourcing companies specialize in their relevant fields and thus have the necessary information and links that are always up to the latest in the market.

Be Helpful

Most times feedback is encouraged and even required to ensure the best possible results are derived from any given endeavor. The feedback whether helpful or not should encompass arrears like progress, material, systems, information and many others.

The feedback can be made in the form of positive, negative, or neutral ratings or comments which it centered on the project itself. Feedback should not be on any other non relating elements as this would be a waste of time and resources.

Helpful feedback is normally done with the inclusion of relative points done in a simple and precise format. Upon reassessing the given feedback information the client is able to assess the immediate repercussion and direction of the project at hand.

Positive feedback can help the team working on the project to feed that their contributions are well received and this will help to further edify their commitment to the project at hand.

Besides the actual feedback which should be as factual as possible, the out sourcing company can also be of even further assistance by providing good and sound advice to their clients.

Again this is helpful to the client who may not be very well equipped in the present chosen endeavor.

For the most part this helpful feedback is done without any fees charged and so it works to the benefit of the client. In providing this possible extra benefit the out sourcing company is also able to sow the seeds of confidence in its capabilities in providing the best services possible.

Chapter 10:
The Dangers Of Not Understanding How To Outsource Correctly

Synopsis

There are several factors why most companies have decided to outsource their work. Among the most prominent reasons are to cut cost and to reduce the dependency on direct employment.

What Can Happen

Understanding the fundamentals tagged to out sourcing is most important to both the customer and the service provider. With the current in sight and information available it is now easier to make a more informed decision as to whether it is a suitable or viable option to elect.

Unfortunately the majority of companies deciding to outsource the bulk of their work load has been done with ill equipped information. As stated the primary reason for out sourcing is to cut cost. However a lot of companies have now found that though out sourcing may contribute to cost cutting, it has also proven to be disadvantageous in other ways. Most of the cost cutting has only short term benefits which eventually contribute to long term problems. These problems may include loss of control over the general business direction, initial options chosen eventually found to be less than suitable, inflexible circumstances are just a few initial problems encountered.

Perhaps the companies that are currently considering the out sourcing option should be asking themselves some serious questions regarding the motive of choosing this particular option. Acknowledging the reasons for choosing out sourcing is a start to understanding the motivation and wisdom or lack of it.

Wrapping Up

The first thing to consider about outsourcing is whether this option is chosen because the idea is to create a condition where the company can concentrate on upgrading their commitments to their customers or is it simply to lessen the current work load and which is intended to create a more cost efficient circumstances. Another fact worth considering is whether or not the out sourcing exercise will benefit in a long term way rather than just short term.

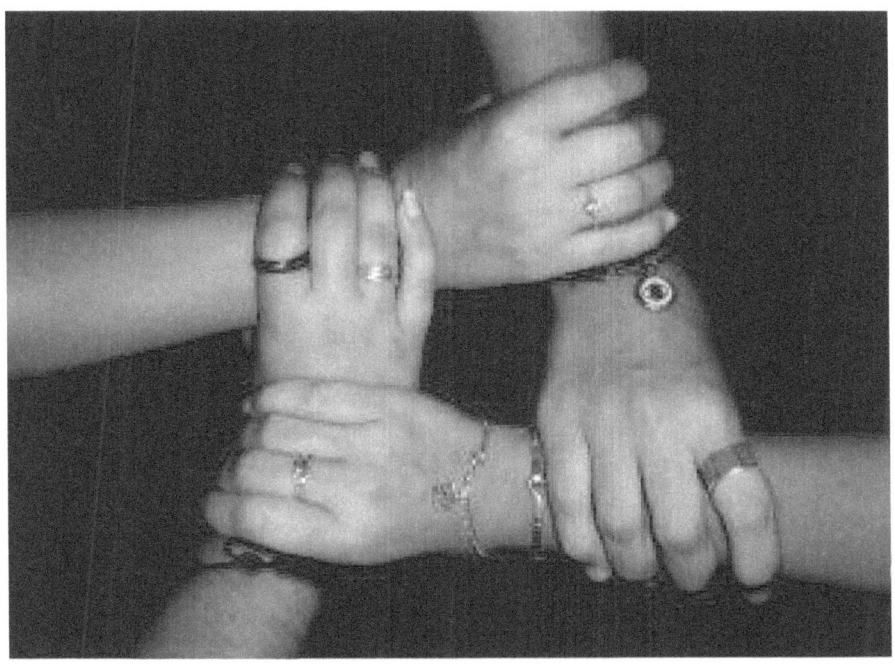